To Vaughn and Nicole
May all your dreams
come true!
Create Your Culture!

Jack Simon

CREATE YOUR CULTURE

CREATE YOUR CULTURE

How to Live a Happy Life
Follow Your Dreams
Turn Ideas into Reality

JACK SIMON

POSITIVE VIBRATIONS

Create Your Culture
How to Live Happy, Follow Your Dreams, Turn Ideas Into
Reality

Published in the United States by Positive Vibrations
Publishing via IngramSpark

1. Self-realization 2. Self-actualization (Psychology)
3. Quality of Life. 4.Self-Help 5. Motivational
6. Creative Nonfiction

www.createyourculturebook.com
www.createyourcultureblog.com

Cover photo by Amanda Elise

ISBN Print: 978-0-9971315-0-5
ISBN eBook: 978-0-9971315-1-2
ISBN Audiobook: 978-0-9971315-2-9

Table of Contents

INTRODUCTION 1

WHAT DOES CREATE YOUR CULTURE MEAN? 3

CREATE YOUR CULTURE MINDSET 7
  1. Success 7
    Success Mindset 8
    Creating a Successful Lifestyle 9
  2. Gratitude 9
  3. Follow Your Dreams 12
    Don't Wait! 14
  4. The 8 Dimensions of Wellness 16
    Spiritual 18
    Emotional 18
    Intellectual 19
    Physical 19
    Environmental 20
    Financial 21
    Occupational 22
    Social 23
  5. Creative Perspective 23
  6. Law of Attraction 24
    Think Positive 25
  7. Flexibility 28
  8. Attitude 29

KNOW YOURSELF 31
  Your Journey 32
  Your Passion 34

Your Vision 34
Understanding 35
Your Purpose and Reason 36

HOW TO TURN AN IDEA INTO REALITY 37
  1. The Notecard Method 37
    History of the Notecard Method 39
  2. The Magic Board 44
    Using the Magic Board 45
    Step-by-Step 46
  3. Intention 50
    The Power of Affirmations 52
  4. ACTION 54
  5. S.M.A.R.T. Goals 57
  6. Concentration and Focus 61

HOW TO EXPAND YOUR MIND 65
  1. The 4 Stages of Learning 65
  2. Get Out of Your Comfort Zone 66
  3. Travel 67

Final Thoughts 69

Acknowledgements 71

Recommended Reading 73

About the Author 75

INTRODUCTION

First off, thank you so much for picking up this book. I truly believe it will make a difference in your life. My goal is that it leaves a positive impact on you with an even greater lasting impression that empowers you to live a happy life, follow your dreams, and turn ideas into reality.

Second, I would like to say that many of the thoughts and ideas contained herein are not original and I will not claim them as such. Much of this is wisdom I have learned from others and things I have come into contact with, read, or experienced on my journey. I am repeating it here in a way that is comprehensible and organized in order to create a guide for you.

Third, I would like to say that the purpose of creating this book is to motivate and inspire a positive change within you, the reader. It is crafted in such a way that you can apply these ideas to your life immediately. Simple, straightforward, and to the point is how we will get down in this book.

With that said, let's take a trip together!

WHAT DOES CREATE YOUR CULTURE MEAN?

Definition

How does one define this phrase?

To me, it means:

Everyone has a unique ability to make the world a better place.

The phrase came to me in 2012 when I was sitting in a debate between an ex-D.E.A. agent and the former editor of *High Times* magazine. The subject, of course, was cannabis. The *High Times* editor was speaking about the 1960s and the "counter-culture" hippie movement. As he spoke he said within a sentence, "they were creating a culture." Bingo! Those words put together ... they were poetry to my ears. The light bulb went off for me right then. Create Your Culture was born. The phrase has since evolved into the mindset that I bring to you in this book.

So what is your "culture" and how do you "create" it? Your culture is your gift, your passion, what makes you feel alive. By living and pursuing this gift, this passion, this light inside you, you are "creating your culture". Again, this is not limited to the arts or music. You have gifts and passions and when you express and share them, you make the world a better place! By Creating Your Culture, you can always be happy, keep a positive attitude, and contribute to society in a positive way.

Do you play sports? Play sports! Create Your Culture! Do you build things with computers or technology? Do that! Create Your Culture! ☺ The more people share their gifts and talents (unique abilities) with the world the more the world rejoices.

Typically, the dictionary version of the word "culture" is language and arts of a society. I believe culture is much bigger than that, and I believe we all have an active role in creating our culture today, because the times and landscape of the world and our society are always changing. They change because of you. You have the power to Create Your Culture.

"When I was 5 years old, my mother always told me happiness was the key to life. When I went to school they asked me what I wanted to be when I grew up. I wrote down 'happy.' They told me I didn't understand the assignment. I told them they didn't understand life."
– John Lennon

John Lennon rehearses Give Peace A Chance photo by Roy Kerwood

CREATE YOUR CULTURE MINDSET

1. Success
Redefining Success

What is success to you? What is your definition of being successful? Do you have an idea of what life is like when you are successful?

Success is a loaded word that means many different things to many different people. The stereotype of success may be material gain, job promotion, a goal achieved, or reaching a great physical feat (like climbing Everest or performing in a sports tournament). But success can be much greater than this. Success can be taking care of your health, living a happy life, enjoying every moment, positively contributing to your community; whatever one chooses. Everyone has different ideas and definitions of success at different stages in their lives.

I will tell you what the word means to me right now. To me, success is being able to do what you want, when you want, and being happy while doing it. For this reason, I am an entrepreneur. Once you define your own definition of success, a clearer picture will emerge of the path you must take to get there to "achieve" your own success.

"Success is a journey, not a destination." – Steve Jobs

When we think of success, we oftentimes create the image of success in our minds without understanding what it will be like once we have become "successful". Do you see yourself as successful? How will you know when you have achieved "success"? Do you have any indicators of success? What are they? Take a moment to write them down.

Success is really just an attitude, for you can only fail if you give up.

Success Mindset

If you want to, you can be so successful! In fact, you are probably already very successful. Think about this: you woke up this morning—success! You completed a goal—success! You have positive thoughts and good health—success!

You can develop a mindset of success whereby many functions and activities in your daily life become small successes. When you achieve your goals, no matter how small or significant, you are experiencing success. Take notice! Did you plan to buy groceries today? Did you buy them? You did? Success! Celebrate this in the moment to form a mental pattern, or habit, of success.

Creating a Successful Lifestyle

With your newfound success mindset you are prepared to take on the world! Create some new goals and get started creating your successful lifestyle. Whether it's focusing on your health, relationships, spirituality, or bank account, think about what a successful lifestyle looks like to you.

Just because your friends or your parents have an idea of success, it doesn't have to be yours! You are a unique person. Your version of success is, too!

"You measure your success by your ability to help others."
- Anonymous

2. Gratitude

My philosophy is that gratitude is the key to happiness. When you are grateful, your life becomes abundant. With modern technology and conveniences, we sometimes forget how good we have it. The thing about gratitude is anyone can do it. What are you thankful for in your life right now? Your health? Your family? Your friends? New opportunities? The list could continue infinitely.

You see, it is all about *recognizing* and being thankful for everything in your life. You may feel like "life" is getting you down or things are not "going your way". If this is the case, pause for a moment and think about all the things you can be thankful for right now. Even so, you should be thankful for your struggles or difficulties because they are helping you grow. They are teaching you. You are learning. Once we begin to practice gratitude daily, our lives become abundant.

We are all blessed. Indeed, you woke up this morning. Give thanks. Count your blessings. Many times people take for granted things so simple as having two legs and two feet. You ate today? Give thanks.

So how does gratitude produce the key to happiness? Really, gratitude is the art of recognizing how blessed you truly are. When you pause to appreciate what you have, who you are, and all the miracles around you, it is impossible not to feel happiness. The beauty of it all is that there is *always* something to be thankful for. I am very grateful you decided to read this book.

Gratitude is the key to happiness. If you want to be happy, become thankful for everything in your life. You may have heard the term "Count your blessings." That's what it's all about. Being grateful for everything brings incredible joy and abundance into your life. Life is not always easy and there can be struggle. But it's how we *view* our lives rather than what happens in our lives that makes a world of difference. If something is not "going your way" or you're feeling it's just "not your day" or you "woke up on the wrong side of the bed," take notice. There is a lesson within the struggle. Now you can be thankful for your struggle because of the lesson you learn from it. Didn't that flip the script? Now you can become happy anytime you feel like life's not going your way. How? Gratitude.

You can be grateful for the good and the bad, the positive and the negative, the births and the deaths, because it is all part of a greater purpose. Just be thankful for who you are, and all the wonders in your life.

Let's practice a gratitude exercise together.

Repeat these affirmations to yourself.

I am grateful for my health.

I am grateful for my eyes.

I am grateful for my ears.

I am grateful for my nose.

I am grateful for my taste buds.

I am grateful for my fingers.

I am grateful for my toes.

I am grateful for the sun.

I am grateful for the sky.

I am grateful for the birds.

I am grateful for my life.

"A grateful heart is a magnet for miracles." – Ras Linga

There are so many things to be thankful for; I could create an entire book out of just counting blessings. There is *always* something to be thankful for … and it doesn't cost a thing. You can choose any blessings to focus on. The possibilities are infinite. You could count blessings all day. Gratitude is a very simple concept but, when practiced, will bring you an incredible amount of happiness and peace.

3. Follow Your Dreams

As I write this I am moments away from visiting the Pyramids of Giza for the first time. In fact, I can see them and the great Sphinx from my window. What I must say is if you have a calling, follow it. Whatever your dream is that is your soul telling you to move towards it—literally, to follow it. I have dreamed of coming to Egypt for as long as I can remember. It is simply fascinating to me. The history, the culture, and the mystery are so attractive to me. I knew at a young age that I must go. Now I am here and, wow, it is breathtaking. I laughed myself to sleep last night with happiness and joy. Today, I will go inside the Great Pyramid. My spirit is so high from the energy of this place and the alignment I am feeling with my purpose.

Your dreams are unique and not for everybody. I think that the bigger the dream the better. You can only fail if you give up. Never give up. Stay positive. Keep trying.

For example, look at airplanes today. There once was a time when man-made flight around the world was a dream, a pretty audacious one, too. Proposing this idea could mean facing ridicule or even being outcast from the mainstream. But people still dreamt. They thought about the idea of humans flying like birds in the sky as a way to travel and be transported. On December 17th, 1903, the brothers Orville and Wilbur Wright tested their contraption in Kitty Hawk, North Carolina. This contraption became known to the world as the first airplane. Although it didn't fly far, the dream had become a reality. I have been to Kitty Hawk and seen the "runway" the brothers used and to describe it in one word: inspiring.

Fast-forward over 100 years and I would be curious to hear what Orville and Wilbur would say about today's high-speed jets, stealth planes, and gigantic commercial airliners, things they may have never even dreamt of.

People may try to discourage you from living your dreams. Don't worry about them. You just have to smile and thank them for their input. They don't understand your vision. Maybe they never will. It's OK. Don't ever compromise living your dreams because someone doesn't believe your dream is possible. Imagine what happened when the Wright brothers explained their vision to those around them, and how many people thought their idea was ridiculous or a waste of time. Now the brothers are immortalized as pioneers of aviation.

Start today.

Follow your dreams to live the dream.

DON'T WAIT!

"Someday" may never come. There are seven days in the week and someday isn't one of them. Go forth and live your dreams! That is what makes you feel alive! Following your dreams isn't some TV show or Hollywood movie. It is as real as it gets.

You are unique and your dreams don't have to make sense to anyone else. Just do it. Follow that imaginative spark in your being. It will guide you. You'll be surprised when you do decide to pursue that "far off" (as it may seem) dream how quickly you are able to bring it to life! The universe wants you to be alive; truly, it is why you are here! The universe wants you to follow your dreams! Turn them into goals!

Set a time! Do it! Mark a date on your calendar. That thing you always wanted to do wants you to pick a date!

Earl Nightingale said, "Never give up on your dreams because of the time it will take. The time will pass anyways." I reflect on this quote right now as I ride an overnight train from Cairo to Aswan, Egypt. I'm thinking, *Wow, this journey will be a long ten days!* but, also, in ten days sitting at home not much will change. Literally, my life is expanding with these ten days. I always wanted to be here and now I am here.

THAT THING YOU ALWAYS WANTED TO DO? NOW IS THE BEST TIME TO START.

"Reality is wrong. Dreams are for real." – Tupac

4. The 8 Dimensions of Wellness

Wellness is a key ingredient in the Create Your Culture mindset. Becoming aware of the dimensions of wellness can help you enjoy a healthy, prosperous, and abundant lifestyle.

Imagine you are the Sun, the center of the galaxy, with the planets orbiting around you. Now imagine that these planets are also smaller suns, with their own gravitational pulls, but still connected to the one Sun in the center of the galaxy. For this next example, you are the Sun and the smaller suns are the dimensions of wellness.

By becoming aware of these dimensions, you can choose to make conscious decisions to improve your life. If you reach a level of contentment, you can always grow by pushing yourself to your "limits". Challenge yourself. Dream big. You will often find that you are much more capable of doing extraordinary things than you previously thought. You will break past your pre-conceived "limits" and continue to grow and thrive, by design.

Example:

Spiritual

(enlightenment)

Give, love, be kind to people, and you will shine bright. Seek purpose and peace in your life. Recognize greater forces than you. Everything is connected. Are you in tune with your higher self and the laws of the universe? Are you in tune with the Great Spirit?

Practice: Be Love. Give Love. Be Peace. Give thanks. Meditate.

Emotional

(happiness)

Emotional happiness will flow to you when you decide to be happy. How you want to feel is up to you. It's not about what happens to us, but how we react. Even in the saddest situations, we can find something to be thankful for. Do you feel happy? Do you enjoy your life? Are you happy?

Practice: Express gratitude. Smile.

*"Don't worry about a thing, every little thing is
going to be alright."*
– Bob Marley

Intellectual
(growth)

Intellectual growth will flow to you when you embrace learning. Your brain works on the principle of "use it or lose it". Commit to learning every day. You can always learn from others. Everyone's story and life is unique. Now, thanks to the Internet, we are living in an amazing time in history when free information is available on any subject you could possibly imagine. Are you constantly learning? Are you growing in your mind? Do you seek mental growth?

Practice: Read a book. Listen to others. Go somewhere you've never been before.

Physical
(health)

Physical health will flow to you when you routinely eat healthy and get plenty of regular exercise. You will feel awesome and full of energy! Healthy nutrition and a proper workout routine will help to create great physical health and wellness. Focusing on a balance of the other dimensions of wellness will also help your physical health and wellness overall.

Focusing on your health will allow you to become healthier by developing healthier habits.

Do you feel good? Do you feel healthy? Does your body feel healthy? Are you eating a balanced, nutritious diet? Are you exercising regularly?

Practice: Develop a consistent fitness program. Make healthy food choices. Stretch. Breathe. Drink water.

Environmental
(freedom)

Environmental freedom is having the ability to create the life you want to live where you are. It is about being surrounded with positive influences. It is about having the ability to do what you want to do in order to be happy and live your dreams. If you are in an environment that does not encourage this, ask yourself, "What would it take for me to get out of this situation?" What does the environmental freedom look like to you? Is your environment conducive to your overall health?

Practice: Clear your workspace and get organized. Optimize your current location. Seek a better living situation or work situation that's more aligned with helping you reach your goals.

Financial
(wealth)

Financial wealth is founded in financial education. Because schools don't educate you about money, or how to make, keep, and grow it, you must decide to learn this on your own.

As you learn more about money, your financial education will increase. As your financial education increases, you will become more informed, enabling you to make wiser decisions when it comes to managing your money, acquiring and building wealth.

Do you know how to build wealth? Do you have a plan to invest and save?

Practice: Seek information on building assets and creating wealth, managing money, and investment strategies.

Talk to people who have made a lot more money than you. They should know a thing or two.

Occupational (purpose)

Occupational purpose makes your life feel like it's worth living. If you have to work all the time, you should do work that you love and believe in. People that are in tune with their occupational purpose might say they are working their "dream job" or something like that. My parents always told me that if I enjoyed the work I was doing, I would never "work" a day in my life.

Does the work you do make you happy? Do you feel fulfilled after completing a long day at work?

Practice: Think about this: If you could work all day and not get tired, what would you be doing? Think about your passions. Think about all the businesses or jobs related to the things you enjoy. Decide to have occupational purpose.

Social

(interaction)

A healthy amount of social interaction will help your well-being. People you meet can become friends. Friends can be there with you to share your successes and support you in times of need. You can also help friends and let them share their experiences with you.

Do you feel a connection with others? Do you share time with others?

Practice: Call your old friends and catch up with them. Stay in contact with your good friends regularly. Spend time with others.

Hopefully, the dimensions of wellness can help you to live a happier life for years to come!

5. Creative Perspective

Your mind is a powerful canvas for you to paint any landscape on. What you create in your mind, your imagination, you can make move in the physical world. The entire world is full of examples. Literally, practically everywhere you go, and everything you see or encounter in a modern city was first thought up in someone's mind. Government? A thought. Traffic lights? A thought. Grocery store? A thought. The shoes you're wearing? Yep, they started as a thought in someone's mind, too. Only you can decide what you want to think. The cool thing is thinking is free, and you have an infinite amount of energy with which to think.

Anything is possible when you think from a creative perspective. By thinking creatively, you can come up with solutions to problems and transform any situation!

The creative power within you is infinite. You must see life from this perspective. Believe in your creativity and know you are a creative being.

6. Law of Attraction

Your thoughts are energy. Thought power is electric and magnetic.

Think about that for a moment.

Every thought you think and every time you think, you send out waves of energy from your mind in every direction, like rays from the Sun. These waves come into contact with other waves of similar patterns of thought and bounce back to create your reality. Imagine your mind as its own radio station. You broadcast your own frequency day in and day out. Although you don't physically observe your thought waves with your own eyes, the force is present. You don't physically observe the earth's magnetic pull but you know it exists because you see the results of gravity. We don't see our thoughts either, just the results. So be careful what you think about and only focus your thought energy on subjects that you wish to bring into or keep in your life. Focus on happy thoughts ☺.

Thought is a powerful force and your mind is a powerful magnet. You attract what you think about most of the time. What you think you become. Your thought power is arguably one of the strongest forces in the universe. Students of mental science have termed this miracle the "Law of Attraction". By broadcasting your mental frequency like a radio (by thinking thoughts), you attract things to your life that exist on that same frequency. What you seek is also seeking you.

Think Positive
The law does not hear positive or negative, it just hears. For example, if you think, *I don't want to go to the store,* the

frequency you are broadcasting is still, "Go to the store." In order to produce what you want, flip the negative into a positive. It's not that you don't want to go to the store, it's that you want to go to the park! Now when you think, *I want to go to the park,* the frequency becomes "Go to the park." Always keep your thoughts in a positive perspective in order to correctly use your thought powers.

Knowing this, you can consciously decide what to think about in order to create the life you want to live. If you want to be happy, you must think happy thoughts. It's easier to create when you align your mind with thoughts that bring you closer to what you seek to manifest.

Think of a time when you wanted something to happen, or when something you imagined came true! In that moment, you attracted it and it came into your life, just like a magnet. When I first learned about this gift, the magnetic power of thought, I wondered how it was already occurring to me in my life. I began to notice subtleties that made me believe more in this idea that your thoughts can attract. Then, one day, something happened that made me a believer for life.

On this fateful morning I had to meet with one of my college professors to discuss some important deadline. Scholarship opportunities were at stake. The problem was our schedules conflicted, and there was absolutely no way we could possibly meet. E-mail and phone calls were out of the question, and this was the last moment we could communicate before the important deadline. I thought about it the night before, thinking positively, *There's got to be a way...* The next morning I woke up, ate breakfast, stretched, and then went for a run. The run took me about 1.5 miles from the school to an open golf course. I had run this route many times before. But this day was amazing.

As I rounded the corner and headed back to my starting point, I noticed a bus in the far distance stop across the street to let people out. I kept running. A man from the bus stop began to walk across the street. I kept running. I got closer and saw that this man had a similar figure to my college professor. "No, it can't be him, can it?" I kept running. Guess what happened? Our paths crossed. Literally. I had been running this path for weeks and had never seen ANY-ONE get off a bus and walk across the street. Furthermore, I had NEVER seen my college professor anywhere except the classroom before this exact moment. But on that fateful morning, my college professor had decided to walk the 1.5 miles to school, so he took the early bus and was dropped off with enough time to spare for his walk. No way... He walked DIRECTLY into the path that I was running. If I had kept running, we surely would have collided. So there I was, talking with my professor when we both had ridiculously different schedules. I could only explain this through the Law of Attraction.

Observe what you think and how your life is around you. Take stock of your mental movements and become aware of what frequency you are broadcasting. Focus on what you want in a positive way and be prepared to attract what you desire.

7. Flexibility

With growth, you will change. Change is the only constant.

Are you rigid in your ways? Can you go with the flow? Will you allow yourself the freedom to grow? Allow change.

"If you want things in your life to change, you have to change things in your life." – Esther Hicks

Flexibility is your ability to adapt with the changes that come. Think about how flexible you can be right now.

Flexibility will allow new opportunities to come into your life and allow you to continually evolve in a positive way.

8. Attitude

Your attitude is the secret sauce. Your attitude towards your work plays a significant role in bringing your ideas to life and your dreams into reality.

When I was a kid I used to play baseball. In the summertime I attended a baseball camp. One year the camp gave out T-shirts to the attendees that said, "WORK HARD AND GOOD THINGS WILL HAPPEN" in big, bold, orange letters. That phrase has stuck with me since then; I always believe that, when you work hard and have a positive purpose behind your actions, good things *will* happen.

Hustle. Drive. Determination. Passion. Dedication. Commitment. Persistence.

These are elements of your attitude. These elements keep you going when all seems lost and it looks like failure or giving up is an option. No, it's not an option; you just continue. Never give up. That is the attitude of a successful person.

You cannot fail; you can only learn from experience and improve.

"The greater the challenge, the greater the reward."
- Anonymous

I believe in the "work smarter, not harder" attitude taught to me by my father. He always said that you can work with your hands, but you can work with your head, too. There are many ways to provide more value through your mind, rather than with your physical capabilities. Even if you are performing manual labor, there may be many ways to optimize your efforts and get more work done in less time or with less effort. Just think about it.

"Dreams don't work unless you do." – John C. Maxwell

A good song for lifting your spirit into a positive, motivated attitude is Jamaican star, Jimmy's Cliff's, "You Can Get It If You Really Want." I suggest giving it a listen! When I feel like I get stuck, this song helps me remember the big picture and may help you, too.

"Genius is 1% inspiration, 99% perspiration."
– Thomas Edison

KNOW YOURSELF

As the ancients said, "Know Thyself." This, my friend, is a very important key to being able to control your destiny. Do you know who you are? I do not mean a flesh, blood and skeleton human; I mean who are you inside, beyond the skin and bones.

You will not find the answers in school. You will not find the answers on TV. You will not receive the answers from your parents, friends, or peers. Indeed, the answer is within you. It is inside you. It is the essence of your being. It is who you are.

Exercise

To learn more about yourself, you must ask yourself these questions:

"Who am I?" "Why am I here?" "What am I doing?" "What is my purpose?"

The questions are best asked in solitude. Outside distractions are just that—distractions. You will only find the true answer within yourself. Once you awaken to who you really are, you can begin to operate your life according to your true identity.

You have to tune out to tune in.

Your purpose will come alive once you understand yourself. You will begin to experience the world around you as you are. Your journey will make more sense.

You will cease to drift aimlessly through life. In this sense, you are now really *living*. You are now truly *alive*. Buddha said, "All that we have become is the result of what we have thought." Once you know who you are, your mind and thoughts will become more aligned to your true identity and purpose. You will begin to live as your true self. The world around you will become a reflection of your true self, who you are within.

In life you will grow, evolve, and change, but the core of your being will be. A powerful affirmation for when you are feeling in alignment with who you are is, "I am now asserting the mastery of my true self."

Your Journey

Everyone has a different journey. Our journeys are created by the choices we make. You define yourself by your actions, by what you do everyday.

"The soul is dyed the color of its thoughts." – Heraclitus

Exercise

If you were to sit back and grab a blank sheet of paper and write down all the things you wanted to do in your life, you might be surprised at what you come up with. Try it. Just think, if time and money did not matter, what would you want to do? Don't think too hard. Write down the first few things that come to your mind.

What you just wrote down is part of your being and who you are. You are consciously creating your experience on this planet and you have chosen these thoughts. Do you know why? Were you influenced by someone or some form of propaganda? Is it a thought related to your current environment? Have you dreamed about these things since you were a child? Don't know why? It's ok, there doesn't have to be an answer.

Your journey begins in your mind.

Along the way

I believe another reason why we are here is to learn lessons. Learning lessons is part of everyone's journey. When "shit happens" or "life happens" it's because you are experiencing a lesson in the present moment. It's not something to complain about, but rather an experience to learn from. Be aware that miracles are happening all around.

Your Passion

Passion is a key element, a key ingredient, to living a happier life. You have to be passionate about something or else you just exist, never knowing what makes you happy.

Exercise

To find your passion, ask yourself some questions:

What really makes me happy?

What keeps me up late at night or motivates me to get out of bed in the morning?

What have I always been interested in?

What could I work on all day long, not get tired, and be happy at the same time?

Let your heart speak to you.

Your Vision

"If you don't know where you're going, any road will take you there." – Lewis Carroll

Life is about creating yourself. Remember those things you always wanted to do when you were a kid? You're supposed to do them! That's why you're alive! Those are your dreams! If you believe you can achieve them you can! All you have to do is set a goal and work towards it. Turn your dreams into goals and your goals into a game. Have fun with it. This is your life. Stay focused towards your vision.

Understanding

I feel unqualified to speak upon the subject of understanding yourself. Everyone is different. You are the one who knows what this means to you.

Seek to understand yourself. With knowledge of your inner self, you can align your life towards your purpose. Understanding is a second layer of meaning. It is one thing to know, another to understand. Understanding gives you clarity as to your role in the greater existence that we all share. Reflecting can help you learn more about yourself.

Also ask why. Taking time to seek understanding can give you perspective on your journey.

Your Purpose and Reason

Passion, Direction, Understanding → Purpose

Combining everything you just thought, you begin to understand your purpose. You begin to understand your reason for being. You begin to become a clearer and more focused being.

With purpose you walk in light. Time does not exist. You move towards your goals, carried by a strong fire within you. You dance to the rhythm of the universe.

Free Resources

createyourculturebook.com/love
for free downloads from this book!

@createyourculture

HOW TO TURN AN IDEA INTO REALITY

1. The Notecard Method

Here it is, one of my personal secrets to success:

Most nights, before I retire, I write down a list of things to do the next day on a 2.5in x 4in notecard, the same index cards we used to study with in grade school. I write the list in order of importance. That way, when I get up in the morning, I know exactly the tasks ahead of me.

Starting with the most important task first, you instantly take action with the notecard. Keeping the notecard in your pocket, you can pull it out and refer to it throughout your day. This gives you constant guidance and serves as a reminder of your goals. It will definitely help you focus! If you find yourself with "nothing to do" … absurd! Just reference your notecard and you have an easy list of actions that will help you reach your goals quicker.

If you find yourself being "busy" are you actually getting things accomplished? How can you tell? Are they on your notecard? No? Yes? Being busy and being productive are two different things. The notecard method helps you stay productive and weeds out tasks that keep you "busy".

The notecard method creates a massive amount of focus. This focus will help you achieve your goals with great speed!

Oftentimes I will group similar activities as they relate to one another or to a similar time of day when I want to complete the tasks. For example, the notecard may include exercise, followed by snack, followed by a shower. I know you may be thinking, *I don't need to write all that down. I know how to plan my day.* Sure, you may be right. But think about this… After you complete each task, you get to cross it off the list! Some tasks are very challenging!

Crossing these challenging tasks off your notecard upon completion gives way to an almost euphoric experience! You are in joy, happiness, and success! Every time you cross a task off your list, it is a success! Why? Because you just moved one step closer to your goals, or accomplished a goal! Now your day becomes filled with small successes and at the end of the day you have crossed off multiple tasks, making your day a grand success! With each successful day, you live a successful life!

But what if you don't finish all the tasks? Well, some tasks are time-bound and others are not. I would suggest making the time-bound tasks a priority. That way you can be sure to first complete the things that need to be done first.

Whatever tasks are left on your card at the end of the day simply rollover to your next index card! Sure, you may just feel like relaxing some days and that's fine because, with the notecard method, you are always on track!

Pro tip: you can always use the backside of the notecard to take notes on the fly for something you may reference or add to your calendar later on.

History of the Notecard Method

You may be wondering, *How long has this method been around? Where did this originate?* The year is 2011 and I am a 20-year-old college student. I was in the top of my class … for throwing house parties. I continually hosted bonfires and gatherings with live bands, which evolved into a backyard music scene. One day, my neighbor and I were hanging out on the porch and he mentioned a certain prominent music venue had openings for bookings. The venue was the Levitt Shell in Overton Park in Memphis, Tennessee, the actual venue where Elvis Presley had his first public performance. I told my neighbor, "They don't need us. We're just some punks." But then I thought, *What do we have to lose?*

The answer was, of course, absolutely nothing.

So I called a few friends who were in bands, found out their availability, created a lineup and pitched the showcase idea to the venue. Guess what? They decided to give us a shot! Wow! Now we had a chance to legitimize our backyard scene and make it public! Great.

The only problem was that we had never done anything like this before!

This showcase developed into a music festival and we had to act fast in order to produce it. This was our shot. Sink or swim, this was it. Either create an awesome event that occurs successfully or retreat to the backyard in defeat (or debt).

Everything was on the line, including our reputations. For me, failure was NOT an option. We HAD to make this work, regardless of whether or not we knew what we were doing.

If you have ever planned an event, whether it was a wedding, birthday party, or a concert, you'll know there is a LOT to do. Not only is there a lot to do, there is a finite amount of time in which to get all the tasks done before the day of the event. The notecard method became my solution.

I began to write down the tasks that needed to be done

in order of importance. When I began doing this, my life changed. There was order out of chaos and organization where none existed previously. It allowed me to create a successful music festival step-by-step from nothing more than a backyard party scene and a dream. 25 days of writing down tasks and taking action created a new habit for me. After the first festival, I continued to use the strategy of the notecard method to improve my "everyday" life. I still use this method today and it is magically effective.

Using the notecard method to plan Bristerfest in 2013 photo
by Carrie Sanders

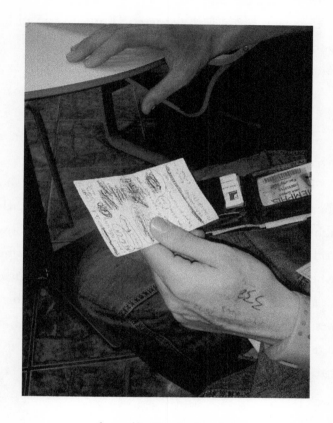

photo by Carrie Sanders

2. The Magic Board

The magic board is the easiest and quickest way I have found yet to manifest an idea in reality. What is a magic board? It is a whiteboard infused with intention.

You may have heard of magic markers or whiteboards, but how about magic boards? When we were kids they gave us magic markers; however, they forgot to mention the power of the magic board.

How does one acquire a magic board? I prefer the shower boards from Home Depot. They are as big as a wall. Their original purpose is actually creating a wall for your shower, but that is not how we use them. The material is the same as a whiteboard yet costs significantly less. The shower boards cost around $15 for something like 8ft x 5ft of whiteboard! Awesome. If you don't have access to Home Depot, any whiteboard will do. Just know, the bigger your board the more space you will have on your board for ideas.

So how does one transform this normal whiteboard into a magic board?

Through our intentions and beliefs.

I believe my shower boards are magical.

I believe I can create my reality through them.

I believe that what I write on the magic board can and will manifest in my reality.

Before you think I'm crazy, let me explain the metaphysics. To start, before I write ANYTHING on the board, the first thing I ALWAYS do is write in the top, left hand corner: "This is a magic board."

This <u>instantly</u> sets my intentions with the board's use and purpose. The board transforms, vibrating with magical powers. These are my beliefs. That's how you transform a normal board into a magic board. By setting your intent for and belief about the board, you transmute the vibrational energy of the board.

Now let me explain how the board is used.

Using the Magic Board

Think about this. You have ideas and thoughts, dreams, or goals in your head. They exist on a mental plane, etheric, and non-physical. To manifest your ideas and thoughts into reality, something physical or tangible, you can use the magic board as a medium.

Think about this. The moment you write your idea down on the magic board, it has instantly become a reality. Literally. You just took something that did not exist on a physical dimension and made it physical, simply through the creative act of writing.

Now just take a step back and observe what you just wrote.

You are now visualizing your idea as it exists in reality. This visualization reinforces the power that exists, working towards bringing your idea to life.

STEP-BY-STEP

1. THINK

2. CREATE

3. VISUALIZE

It really is that simple.

Don't ask me if it works; I know it works. I have had unbelievable things happen in my life that all began as thoughts transcribed on a magic board. You must believe in the power of the board or it will not work.

I have friends who have tried to use the board to no avail. I have also had friends who discovered the wonderful power of the board, the magic phenomena, and began to implement it in their lives. Sometimes action is required to turn your ideas to reality and sometimes it is not. Just allowing your ideas to flow to you and being in tune with what you want can be enough sometimes. Coincidence?

No. Alignment? Yes. Being in tune is being in alignment with your purpose.

I remember one of my friends said he was performing (a musician) and afterwards people asked him for his autograph. I thought that was cool and decided to write on my board that morning, "I want someone to ask me for my autograph." Literally, less than 6 hours later, I was on a plane and the person next to me asked me for my autograph! No shit. This never happens. I hadn't even mentioned *anything* about the board and what I had written on it earlier. To that person, it just happened. And it happened very organically in conversation.

During the writing of this book, a friend stopped by my house and was expressing how she wanted to go to a certain music festival. I told her to write it down on the magic board. Within three days of writing down her intention on the magic board, "I want to go to Art Outside," she had acquired a free ticket. Don't ask me if it works! You have to believe.

The fact is that whatever you wish for can come true and can come true a lot faster with the help of a magic board. A lot of times I use it to develop ideas, which are then broken down into tasks and simple steps of action for the notecard! So combining the Magic Board and the Notecard Method is a way to design your life through your creative thought and action. Guess what I wrote on my board recently? "Write." What am I doing now? Writing this book… Now my board reflects my reality; it says, "Write your book!" ☺

3. Intention

Intention is all about conscious creation. Intention sets the stage to help you turn your idea into reality on a mental plane. When you decide what you want, you emit a vibe that attracts what you want to you. Intention moves you towards your goal through purpose. There is a reason why you want what you want. There is a reason why you want to turn your idea into reality. This reason is the motivating force behind the purpose that guides your intention. Tap into it. Become friends with it. Know your reason, know your purpose, and set the intention. It will bring what you want closer to you, faster.

"Our intention creates our reality." – *Wayne Dyer*

Have you ever been thinking about something and then started to notice a lot more of it? Just by your thoughts, you've brought that thing closer to you. Intention brings attention. Where attention goes, energy flows. When you set your attention on your intention, cosmic forces move in accordance with it. This will help you turn your ideas into reality.

"All that matters is if someone is a good person."
— My dad, Kent Simon

Positive or negative, the choice is yours, but I believe you have to set a positive intention to really work with the energy. When the intention is positive, honest, and pure, amazing things will happen. You are a magnet to what you place your attention on. Focus on the positive.

Exercise: Let's set the intention to be happy right now.

Be happy in this moment. This moment is your life. Feel happiness. Focus on what makes you happy! Do what it takes to be happy right now. Express your gratitude. What makes you happy right now?

Think about it.

Wow, aren't you feeling happy now? Think about your body language. Did it just change in any way? Are you smiling? ☺

Body language can help guide your intention because your body language is how you outwardly express your inner self. If it's a certain mood you're trying to experience, how does your posture reflect that? Smiling is always a good thing, too.

The Power of Affirmations

To experience the full power of intention, you can embed thoughts into your own subconscious mind with affirmations that align with your intent.

Your subconscious mind is the active mind that is always working. It is what keeps you alive. You aren't consciously telling yourself to breathe right now or pump blood from your heart, are you? That's your subconscious mind operating right now and it controls your bodily functions and habits.

Affirmations are statements that you can use to program the beliefs of your subconscious mind. Affirmations can be used to control your habits and help you turn your ideas into reality or bring you closer to your dreams.

When you repeatedly give attention to certain thoughts, you form mental habits. When these habits become strongly engrained in your way of thinking to the point where you don't think about them, you know or believe, you have *turned your habit into a belief.*

At the point when a habit becomes a belief, you have successfully taken an idea and embedded it into your mind to the point where it has now become part of your mental process. It will become easier for you to attract the things you want through your intention, because you believe it is possible.

Exercise:

Think of a thought you would like to turn into a belief.

Write down a *positive* statement related to that, starting with "I am."

For example, "I am full of energy," as opposed to, "I am not tired." Remember to focus on what you want in a positive way.

Make sure you feel good about it. Does it feel right to you when you say it? When you do, it works miracles. When you don't, it won't work right.

"I am the master of my destiny," is one of my favorites. It always feels good to me. I believe it.

4. ACTION

When I traveled Europe in 2012 I made a short inspirational video at several sites including the Eiffel Tower in France, the Colosseum in Italy, and Stonehenge in England. My words from the video still reflect how I feel about action:

"You can do anything you want in life, but it's going to require energy and action.
Start by creating a goal in your mind. Then visualize yourself having already attained that goal. What does it look like? What does it feel like?
The answers to those questions will give you a clear idea of the results you seek.
Write them down and reference them daily.
Now take action towards that result every day with focus, desire, passion, determination, confidence, and willpower.
Remember our creative ability is infinite and that dream you have is meant to be realized."

Action is what separates the talkers from the doers.

"You don't have to be great to start, but you have to start to be great."
– Zig Ziglar

We've all met someone who says they've got plans to do this or plans to do that, but they never actually take action towards any of them. Please don't let yourself be that person! Don't even tell people you're going to do something if you have no intention of actually doing it. There's no point. You're wasting your breath and their time. Let your actions speak for you. Just do it. Talk about it later after it's already done. *What you do* always says more about *who you are* than *what you say*. Sure, it is fine to discuss ideas and talk about things we can create or develop, but you don't want to become someone who is always talking and never doing. As my friend Trey said, "Your mouth and your feet have to do the same thing."

Strive to be a person of action. Strive to follow through on your dreams and endeavors until the finish.

"Do or do not. There is no try." - Yoda

A famous statement decrees "knowledge is power." So if you have knowledge, you have power, right? Wrong. The key is in applied knowledge. Applied knowledge is the real power. Napoleon Hill said, "Action is the real measure of intelligence." If you can take what you know and apply it, you can create the life you want to live.

THE DISTANCE BETWEEN YOUR DREAMS AND REALITY IS CALLED ACTION

If you take nothing else from this book, just remember to take action towards your goals and dreams every day. Faith will not move the mountain alone. You must take action.

"Words may show a man's wit, but action his meaning."
– Ben Franklin

5. S.M.A.R.T. Goals

"A goal is a dream with a deadline." – Napoleon Hill

American self-help writer Napoleon Hill (1883-1970) posing for a portrait

That's one of the most powerful sentences I've ever heard. What Napoleon Hill says is that you can literally turn your dreams into goals.

Many people have bucket lists, wish lists, or fantasies about what they "would want to do" with their life. Me?

I've got to-do lists, action lists, or lists of things "I will accomplish" in life. Why write a bucket list? Why not write a to-do list and commit yourself to living your dreams? It's totally possible. Let me share with you a way to help map out a plan towards achieving your dreams. You will be able to turn your dreams into achievable S.M.A.R.T. goals after this chapter!

S.M.A.R.T. is an acronym used to help fine-tune a goal into an action plan. Business management books popularized the acronym in the 1980s. Since then it has evolved, and many words have been used in the S.M.A.R.T. acronym. This is the version I stuck with. I'm not sure where I was first exposed to this idea, but it has been a very beneficial tool for me for years.

What is a S.M.A.R.T. goal?

A goal that is:

Specific

You want to be as specific as possible about your goal so you know when you have achieved it.

Measurable

Quantify your goal so that you can track everything. This will keep you on time.

Action-Oriented

You need to be able to take action towards your goal. You will lose time and energy if there is not a way for you to take action.

Results-Oriented

What is the ultimate result? Identify the result and your goal will become easier to attain.

Timebound

Set a date. Write it down on the calendar. Now commit to it.

Now that we've seen the acronym, let's look at an example of how to create a S.M.A.R.T. goal. We'll start with an idea and transform it into a S.M.A.R.T. goal to make it happen!

For this example, let's say you want to travel. Say you want to go to Europe. More specifically, you want to go to the Netherlands because you've always wanted to go to Amsterdam and see what's up with the coffee shops.

That's the vague goal or idea where you start. Now transform it into a S.M.A.R.T. goal.

You want to spend 1 week in Amsterdam, October 20-27, visiting the 3 specific museums, exploring the city, enjoying live music and going to at least 3 specific coffee shops. You figure out the budget and decide it's going to cost you $2500 in flights, hotels, food, etc. and you figure out how you are going to acquire the necessary funds. You'll know you've achieved your goal when you're walking among the beautiful canals, eating kebabs, enjoying the sights, sounds, and smells.

Using the S.M.A.R.T. goal design, you can make your dreams a reality much faster than just wishing or thinking about vague goals.

Inspiration

5. Concentration and Focus

Concentration is a key ingredient in success.

In order to concentrate, you must eliminate distractions.

Concentration is directing your mind's energy, your thoughts, towards a specific subject. Focus is the center of interest or activity.

Concentration and focus work together. When you concentrate on an idea, and focus your actions on a specific task, you can maintain continual progress.

It is important that you spend time each day focusing your intention on your goals. Concentrate on them for a few minutes before thinking other thoughts.

Concentration helps amplify the powers of the Law of Attraction. The stronger mental vibration you emit, for the longer period of time, the more prevalent the vibration becomes in your reality. Concentration helps you build energy towards a specific desired outcome.

By focusing your intention on the desired outcome you wish to achieve, you invest your mental energy in the creation of that outcome.

Focus is about keeping your attention in tune with your objective for the time that it takes to create or successfully achieve the goal.

EXERCISE:

A powerful method of concentration is attributed to one of the most famous thinkers, Albert Einstein. The Distraction Index can help you become stronger at concentrating, whether Einstein actually used this method or not.

As the story goes, when Albert was thinking, he would have a sheet of paper lying next to him. If something were to distract him from his focus, he would write on the paper "_____ will not distract me again." For example, if the birds chirping outside distracted him, he would write, "The birds chirping will not distract me again." He would think about this for a moment and then return to his work. Over time, he was able to achieve an incredibly powerful ability to concentrate and focus, because nothing could distract him anymore. He was completely utilizing all of his mental energy in creating the solution or solving the problem.

You can use this method to develop and achieve your own powerful concentration.

Albert Einstein during a lecture in Vienna in 1921 by the portraitist F. Schmutzer

Focusing becomes easier and easier when you're working with your purpose and you're passionate about the work you are doing. You could become lost in work for hours, only to realize, "Oh yea, we need to stop and get some food!" By doing what you love, you can focus an incredible amount of your energy towards achieving your goals.

HOW TO EXPAND YOUR MIND

1. The 4 Stages of Learning

This is an idea a friend exposed me to in 2012. It breaks down your understanding of any subject into four different stages. When you are aware of the four stages of learning, you can better educate yourself by understanding where you are in the process.

<u>The 4 Stages of Learning:</u>
1. Unconscious Incompetence
2. Conscious Incompetence
3. Conscious Competence
4. Unconscious Competence

Let me give you an example so this will make sense. Imagine a drum.

You begin learning with unconscious incompetence. Before you knew what a drum was, you had unconscious incompetence, because *you didn't even know* what a drum *was*, let alone how to play it.

Once you find out that drums exist, you become conscious of them. You are aware of what the drum is, yet you still don't know how to play it. You are in the stage of conscious incompetence.

As you learn how to play the drum, you become conscious and competent. You know how to play the drum. You are aware of the drum. You have learned what the drum is and how to use it to make music.

After you practice and practice, committing your rhythms to muscle memory, you no longer need your sheet music or music instructor as a guide. You feel comfortable enough to play the drum without thinking. You know what you're doing and don't have to concentrate hard on it but can still create the right rhythm with precision. Upon reaching this stage, you have developed unconscious competence.

Now that you are aware of the four stages of learning, you can apply the idea to your life to help you learn and grow.

Learning is a gift. Commit yourself to being a lifelong learner.

2. Get Out of Your Comfort Zone

"A ship in the harbor is safe, but that is not what ships are built for." – William Shedd

A great way to expand your mind is by getting out of your comfort zone. It has the power to change your life.

As humans, we tend to build our little nests where we feel comfortable. But staying in your comfort zone can make one complacent and inhibit the potential to learn and grow from new things that exist outside the personal space.

Go on an adventure. Take a different route home. Go explore a place you've never been. By placing yourself in a new environment, you will soak up new information and expand your mind.

Which leads me to my next point...

3. Travel

I believe traveling is one of the easiest ways to expand your mind. You can read about a place, watch movies, or hear what your friend who's been there thinks about it, but there is nothing like actually going somewhere completely foreign or new to you and becoming immersed in the surroundings. Just being there, your subconscious mind will immediately begin absorbing and interpreting the new information and stimulation.

Meeting people when traveling is always important. You can learn so much from people all over the world. Everyone has a story to tell. Everyone has an idea, a gift, or a message to share.

By listening and tuning in to an environment that is completely new to you, your knowledge and understanding of many things will grow. Your mind will expand simply by being exposed to new places and concepts while traveling.

I would encourage you to travel.

Final Thoughts

"The people who are crazy enough to think they can change the world are the ones who do." — Steve Jobs

It really all comes down to choices. Your life is a continuum of choices. What will you do with your time on this earth? I hope the lessons taught in this book will guide and give you strength on your journey and continually benefit you throughout your life.

I believe you have the power within you to become the happiest person alive. You were born to follow your dreams. You *can* turn your ideas into reality.

Enjoy the moment. Be at Peace. Live, Love, Laugh, Be Grateful.

Be a force for something good.

There are no excuses. Do not attempt to justify your failures. Only learn and progress.

So here we are now. Don't hold back.

Free Resources
createyourculturebook.com/love
for free downloads from this book!
@createyourculture

Thanks for reading. If you enjoyed this book, you can visit my blog at http://www.createyourcultureblog.com for more ideas, inspiration and adventure.

I'd love to hear your story! Write to me at createyourculture@gmail.com and tell me how this book impacted your life!

One Love.

ACKNOWLEDGEMENTS

Love and Gratitude

Thanks to Jared Williams for inspiring me to write this book. He told me I had some good ideas that would help other people if I wrote them down and shared the philosophy. Thank you, Jared.

Thanks to Amanda Elise for taking the cover photo in Egypt.

Thanks to Irina Doroshenko, amazing artist who painted an incredible photo for me to use, and special thanks to Frank Chin for taking the original photo.

Thanks to Hagit Hikry for reading the first few paragraphs as I scribbled them down on my notepad and encouraging me to finish what I started.

Thanks to my friends who helped read preliminary copies and give me their in-depth feedback including Tim Stanek, Michael Shelton, and Chris Warnock.

Thanks to the Brister Street and Brister Fest community and Memphis, Tennessee, which has allowed me to create culture and live my dreams.

Thanks to everyone who read this book including YOU.

Thanks to God for allowing me to live another day.

Thanks to my mother, Annette, and my father, Kent, who I love beyond all things that are real.

To all my friends and family across this world, keep the light.

Recommended Reading

Here is a list of recommended books to help you live a happier life, follow your dreams, and turn ideas into reality.

Coelho, Paulo. *The Alchemist*. San Francisco: Harper San Francisco, 1993. Print.

Bristol, Claude M. *The Magic of Believing*. New York: Prentice-Hall, 1948. Print.

Templeton, John. *Worldwide Laws of Life*. Philadelphia: Templeton Foundation, 1997. Print.

Hill, Napoleon. *The Law of Success*. New York: Jeremy P. Tarcher/Penguin, 2008. Print.

Murphy, Joseph. *Power of Your Subconscious Mind*. New York, NY: Bantam, 1982. Print.

About the Author

<u>Jack Simon</u> is an artist, philosopher, and entrepreneur with a passion for music and travel.

In 2015 he launched an electronic press kit service, <u>EPKpage</u>, to help artists and musicians look more professional online in order to get booked and perform at more venues and festivals.

He is the Founder and Creative Director of <u>Brister Street Productions</u> and <u>BristerFest</u>. His production company has hosted or co-produced hundreds of events and festivals and half a dozen music videos, helped raise over $9310 for non-profit causes and over 1,000 pounds of canned goods for food banks from 2011-2015.

When Jack was 5 years old, his younger sister passed away at the age of 3. His thoughts were published in a book detailing a child's perspective on death, _This Book Is For All Kids But Especially My Sister Libby. Libby Died._, which has since been translated and published internationally in Japan.

He grew up immersed in the weird, live music playground known as Austin, Texas. In 2008 he moved to Memphis, Tennessee where he currently lives and creates.

He writes at www.createyourcultureblog.com and you can connect with him on Facebook and instagram @createyourculture and facebook.com/createyourculture.